The Flowers Before They Bloom
By Devona Fayana

The Flowers Before They Bloom

Copyright 2020 © by Devona Fayana Nelson

All rights reserved. No part of this publication may be reproduced in any form without permission in writing from the author.

Book cover by Devona Fayana

Scripture quotations are from The ESV® Bible (The Holy Bible, English Standard Version®), copyright © 2001 by Crossway, a publishing ministry of Good News Publishers. Used by permission. All rights reserved.

ISBN 9798640658316 (Paperback Edition)

To my Beloved Redeemer and Best Friend. The One who healed, nurtured and blossomed me into wholeness, securely planted in the palm of His hands.

Contents

Rising	13
Pruning	39
Budding	71
Blossoming	93
Letters In Bloom	107
Acknowledgements	167

"Gracious words are like a honeycomb,
sweetness to the soul and health to the body."

- Proverbs 16:24

Introduction

The burden was so potent within me when the Lord placed it on my heart to create a beautiful written piece of work dedicated to encouraging His wonderful daughters.
God's love for us is magnificently great and the depth of His love towards His daughters exceeds beyond our comprehension. I created The Flowers Before They Bloom in obedience to God in order to uplift the hearts of women through beautiful words of encouragement that is inspired by the glorious word of God.

As you read this lovely book, I would love for your heart to feel the warmth of His love for you, allow the words to truly absorb into your spirit.

The Flowers Before They Bloom

The Flowers Before They Bloom will take you on a journey of healing and wholeness as you grow in intimacy with the Lord. As a flower flourishes and blossoms into the fullness of what they've been created to be, so it is as the Lord is blooming and cultivating you into fruitfulness within the fullness of your purpose as you abide in His love.

There is beauty and fulfilment as you abide in Christ and His words abide in you, for not only do you experience the wonderful experience of eternal life through knowing His heart intimately, but you also blossom beautifully into the woman that He has created you to be. The Lord longs for you to dwell underneath the shadow of His wings and for you to grow in confidence of your identity and precious value within Him, as He embraces you securely in His loving arms.
God has delightful plans for you, lovely plans for you to give you a prosperous future and a hope. He is your loving protecter, provider and sustainer. I want to encourage you that He is able to provide all of your needs according to His riches in glory, exceedingly and abundantly more than you could ask for or imagine.

The Flowers Before They Bloom

Beautiful woman of God, continue to cling on to the heart of your Beloved Redeemer. When the trials and stormy seasons come, always remain firmly planted in His word, anchored in His truth. For through your unwavering faith and intimacy with the Lord Almighty, greatness will bloom and burst forth in your life. Always remain in His love, being truly connected to the sweet vine and the vinedresser will cause you to produce fruit in your life so beautifully that His magnificent glory will be seen over your precious life.

Whatever you are facing during this season, always know that nothing is impossible with God. May you be strengthened and empowered through the Holy Spirit and remember that you can do all things through Christ. May your heart be blessed and your mind renewed and transformed as you read The Flowers Before They Bloom. May you also bloom beautifully in the hands and heart of your Beloved Saviour, every day of your precious life.
You are forever loved and taken care of by God. Draw nearer to His wonderful heart as He draws closer to you. Keep on blossoming in His steadfast love.

Rising

Taking her by the hand He said to her, "Talitha cumi," which means, "Little girl, I say to you, arise." - Mark 5:41

The Flowers Before They Bloom

When your heart is surrendered to the Lord, He will gradually draw you deeper in relationship with Him, that you may grow more in the knowledge and true revelation of His glorious, unfailing love for you. As you immerse yourself in the depths of His love, the Lord in His faithfulness will uproot some things that have remained within you, that have kept you hindered from blossoming into the woman He has destined for you to beautifully become.

Perfection doesn't exist within us, through which we all have weaknesses and unfortunate events that may have caused us to feel hurt and broken due to previous experiences and circumstances that we have faced. However the Lord is faithful, and He is able to rebuild you and restore all that has been damaged or lost.

When God prepares you to arise higher in strength and fruitfulness, one of the first things you will experience in your journey of blooming is the season of rising. Rising above your past, rising above your heartbreak, above your circumstances and keeping yourself securely rooted and planted in the heart of God.

The Flowers Before They Bloom

As you rise above the things that hinder you, I encourage you to saturate yourself in His presence through worship, prayer and study of His powerful word. Something that helps especially throughout the blossoming journey of our lives is to renew our minds daily. We ought to be transformed through the renewing of our minds, what better way to do it through keeping our minds meditating on the beautiful scriptures.

Through absorbing His word and soaking His presence through lovely worship and praise, we are transformed beautifully by Him. The wonderful thing about the Lord is that He is eternal and His love for us is unfailing. He is gracious and merciful, slow to anger and abounding in steadfast love. Through which you will be confident to know that He will never give up on you. Beautiful transformations and the healing process takes time. But in order for something to flourish in the fullness of it's potential it needs to be nurtured and rooted securely on a firm foundation.

The Flowers Before They Bloom

May you alway nourish your spirit with God's word as He showers you with His love. He will always hold you firmly in His heart. Press deeper into your relationship with God like never before.

The Encounter

His embrace was heavenly.
My hand was clenched firmly in His,
As the strength of His love wrapped over me,
I was truly held secure and tightly gripped,
With the overwhelming beautiful love from
heaven, showering over me.

And from that moment I knew,
That my heart shall forever be intertwined with
Him.
For His grace abounds so potent,
That He purified me and washed me clean,
From the multitude of my sins.

- Devona Fayana

Covered In Grace

Let your heart not be troubled,
Nor let your mind be fearful,
To proceed and arise beautifully,
In resilience, boldness and strength.
May you flourish in your faith,
May you always continue to press forward,
Persevering persistently at your own pace.
For your precious life is dearly cherished,
And is truly covered with His eternal loving grace.

- Devona Fayana

The Flowers Before They Bloom

Today, Tomorrow and Forevermore

He loves you today,
He loves you tomorrow,
He loves you forever,
He loves you at your darkest,
He loves you when you're doing your best,
He loves you no matter what you've done,
He loves you so dearly, that He gave His only Son,
For His love, His goodness, His grace,
And His mercy cannot closely compare to
anyone.

- Devona Fayana

Love Cravings

It is clear that you crave a love so deep,
Deeper than the depths of the oceans,
And higher than the heavens above.
Though there is a truth you need to know,
That there is no height, nor depth,
Nor life nor death,
Nor things present, or the things to come,
Will be able to separate you from the love of God.
For His glorious love is truly unfailing,
And every inch of craving of love,
That you are grasping to feel,
You will experience it exceedingly and abundantly,
More than you can ask of or imagine.
For God is able,
To love you,
And satisfy your every need.

- Devona Fayana

The Flowers Before They Bloom

Exceedingly and Abundantly

He will replace every piercing wound in your heart,
With the precious overflow of His glorious love.
For the Redeemer of your soul is truly able,
To heal you, and protect you with wonderful love and care from heaven above.
He shall exceed your expectations,
And succeed beyond your hearts most deepest desires.

For there is nothing,
that you can ask for,
or imagine,
That he is unable do.
May you receive,
Exceedingly and abundantly,
More than you've ever dreamed of in this world.

- Devona Fayana

The Flowers Before They Bloom

Bloom Where You Are Planted

He uproots the weariness,
He digs deep into your worries and cares.
He carves through the darkest places of your soul
and pulls out all the shattered heart pieces that
were hidden.
He kisses away every trace of you that was broken
in your midst.
He will find the muddiest places of your heart,
And plant the most beautiful, glorious garden of
flowers.
He will tell you that you are beautiful,
And that His splendour is clothed all over you,
Like the exquisite lilies of the field.
For His grace is sufficient,
To blossom you as whole, healed and beautiful,
firmly planted in His hands.
You will always be lovely,
And you will always be beautiful to Him no
matter what.
Even after all your moments of darkness and
weakness.

- Devona Fayana

The Flowers Before They Bloom

Beauty In The Madness

Refrain your lovely eyes,
from flooding tears of sorrow.
For soon your eyes shall be filled,
With the overwhelming light of freedom,
wholeness and joy.
The Lord is surely able,
To bring you transformation out of dull places,
And beauty from the ashes.

Do not be dismayed,
The mess will transition to a powerful message of greatness and resilience.
For what the enemy used to destroy you,
Shall be transformed for God's glory.
And the abundance, protection and wellbeing of your precious life.
For you are greatly adored and cherished in the arms of your Beloved.
Forever and always,
He is restoring and transforming you.
Gloriously, exquisitely, remarkably.

- Devona Fayana

Restore Your Petals

He is restoring your strength,
Through the beauty of praise that clothes you,
With great force of persistence and resilience,
And the strong armour of God that upholds you,
to carefully withstand the storms.

The battles that you have faced,
May have tested you just for a moment,
But once the rainfall has passed,
Your petals shall blossom beautifully in greatness,
In glory and the splendour of strength.
Better and more refined than never before.

- Devona Fayana

The Flowers Before They Bloom

Spring Season

Beloved your time of glory has come,
For the season of your barrenness is over,
And the wilderness experience has come to an end.
For God shall bring glorious transformation of blessing to you.
May your wilderness become like the garden of Eden,
And the produce of your life be flourishing in the fullness of fruitfulness that has been destined to spring forth in your life.

- Devona Fayana

The Flowers Before They Bloom

Flourishing Hope

Never be dismayed, nor fix your thoughts on the things that were before.
Set your heart on the beautiful hope, that you soon will experience,
The blossoming season of prosperous promises soon to come,
For God has precious plans for you,
To provide you with a flourishing future.
So refrain from giving up, nor giving in to doubt.
For as you flourish in your faith,
Your life will blossom and unfold,
beautifully and gracefully in success.
More than you asked for or could've even imagined.

- Devona Fayana

The Flowers Before They Bloom

Beauty In Transformation

There is beauty in change,
And grace in seasons of transformation.
The previous conditions of your heart,
Does not determine the sensational transfiguration,
That will flourish through every part.
He will heal and restore,
All that you have lost.
And the beauty of it all,
Is that though His grace, you are redeemed.
He loves you greatly,
He was willing to save you,
At such dear cost.

- Devona Fayana

The Flowers Before They Bloom

To Blossom

As you are firmly planted fearfully and wonderfully,
In the arms of your creator,
May you be filled and satisfied by the fountain of life,
Watering and comforting you, through the outpouring of His Spirit.
As His light glistens gloriously over you,
May the warmth of His love,
And the indwelling of His presence,
Overflow from within you.
Through which your your petals shall blossom,
And your heart will flourish,
Beautifully and exquisitely, now and forevermore in His hands.

- Devona Fayana

Magnificent Mind

There is potent power in your thoughts,
And true wonder in the words that you say.
God has formed your mind in such a way,
That it's magnificent, and has the ability,
To have an effect on your life in many, various ways.
Be transformed by the renewal of your mind,
Align your words with His,
And in true joy and peace within fruitfulness,
Is your portion that you shall always pleasantly live.

- Devona Fayana

The Flowers Before They Bloom

The Stormy Seasons

The battles that you faced,
On the frontline,
Of stormy seasons,
Was not to destroy you,
But to prune and refine you.
For without rain,
There are no flowers.

- Devona Fayana

The Flowers Before They Bloom

The Rising Rose

The lone rose blossoms in her field,
She flourishes in her faith,
Expectant that her provider will nourish and protect her,
That she may blossom beautifully in due time.
She understands that all flowers bloom differently,
And that all the plants of the field are wonderfully unique.
She rises faithfully each day,
For it is the strength and persistence deposited in her,
That keeps her petals still flourishing boldly and beautifully,
Each and every single day.

- Devona Fayana

Lovely Life

I can imagine for such a long time,
You may have desired,
A pleasant, care-free lovely life,
The life that consists of no anxiety and no experiences of heartbreak.
But through Christ there is fullness of love filling every empty space in your heart,
With the abundance of joy, gracing you with precious moments of life.
This is written to tell you that all these beautiful things are available to you,
Everything that is lovely and is rooted of the fruitfulness of joy is given to you,
Through His abundant grace.
For He is able, to stay true to His Word,
For He is mighty to save.

- Devona Fayana

Rooting and Rising

The beauty of life is to fear the Lord and grow deeper within His love,
To also know that your roots do not always truly determine,
The risen place of your divine destination.
For where you currently are,
Does not determine where you are going.
Life is a journey,
Destiny isn't a destination.
It's all a process.
Everyday you are rising from your roots,
And blossoming beautifully with progress.
May you rise strong,
And bloom gracefully where you are planted.

- Devona Fayana

Pure Redemption

The guilt and the shame,
is no longer your portion.
For Christ has redeemed you,
And given you a new name.
He has marked you as His own,
Through His precious, incorruptible blood.
Through His stripes you are healed.
And over your life, the glory of God shall be revealed.
You are sanctified and purified beloved one,
through the wonderful beauty
and power of His unchanging Word.

- Devona Fayana

The Flowers Before They Bloom

Planted

You may feel as though,
that you have been buried in the dirt.
But truly, you have been planted in good soil,
To preserve you and hide you,
As you are being prepared for greater things so wonderful and great, beyond your imagination.
For all that you have experienced, will not go in vain.
But you must hold on strong and be hopeful,
As you trust that God will send you the glorious rain.
May you may bloom where you have been planted,
For there is a light shining on the horizon.
And as you arise, the rain of refreshing better days will come flooding through.
So sit tight, seasons are only for a moment,
But you will forever be firmly planted in His hands.

- Devona Fayana

The Flowers Before They Bloom

Treasure In Petals

Beloved, you are fearfully and wonderfully made.
For the petals of your heart's purpose were
formed beautifully diverse.
Refrain from pointing out your differences,
And embrace the beauty of your path and
individuality.
For a flower is never identical to another,
But they all still bloom and blossom beautifully
in their own ways.
According to the faith that resides within them,
And the nourishment and strength of their roots.
Let the roots of your heart be strengthened and
encouraged,
Through the watering of His Word.
May your faith arise and flourish in awe and
wonder. For the treasure you've always sought,
Lays right in your heart.
There is purpose and power residing within you.
God has given you the ability to flourish in
fruitfulness, faith and abundance of love.
Choose faith to flourish every day.

- Devona Fayana

Surrendered

It's been far from easy throughout this season,
But you've always given me a reason,
To hold on,
And what would be a better reason,
To live for you,
Because you died for me.

- Devona Fayana

Pruning

I am the true vine, and my Father is the vinedresser. Every branch in me that does not bear fruit he takes away, and every branch that does bear fruit he prunes, that it may bear more fruit. - John 15:1-2

The Flowers Before They Bloom

You are resiliently rising as the Holy Spirit strengthens you to bloom forward, further into your beautiful destiny to become more fruitful pursuing God's will.

Although as you remain steadfast and abide faithfully within the Lord, once He sees the wonderful fruit that you bear, He will begin to prune you so that you will bear more fruit. The pruning season throughout your blossoming journey is probably one of the most challenging moments to experience. This is due to the removal process. God will begin to remove certain strongholds, patterns and emotional and spiritual bondages that keep us hindered from being the whole person that He wants us to be.

This difficult process is not to harm you, but to take care of you, protect you and cause you to grow more fruitfully. Just as a flower may be pruned by a gardener in order for it to grow bigger, healthier and better than before, so it is when the Lord is pruning and taking care of us.

The Flowers Before They Bloom

The experience may sometimes feel like you're in the wilderness, and sometimes you may get those times where you feel discouraged but I want you to be encouraged, to know that the season you are experiencing will not go in vain.

In order for you to move forward within every area of your life, work needs to be done from within our hearts. Nobody is perfect, and there is always work and growth to be done within us all.

Although I truly see the pruning season as a time of acceleration. Almost like a growth spurt. An accelerated season of preparation for increase, maximisation and fruitfulness. Therefore do not be dismayed, for God is moulding you for something beautiful.

There is power and transformation in these precious moments of your life. It is within these times that contribute to you becoming the person God has destined for you to become. It prepares you to fulfil your purpose and walk in the fullness of your calling. May God show you with clarity the beautiful work that He is doing in your heart in this season, so you will be truly encouraged.

Stripped

He strips you of everything that has ever
hindered you.
Every feeling, every emotion, every stronghold,
every setback.
He uproots from the depths of your soul,
All that has held you back,
Shall now be demolished and crumbled right
before you,
For God is your sovereign healer,
And He who is the restorer of all,
Is faithful to strip darkness off you,
And position you into the radiance of His light.

- Devona Fayana

The Flowers Before They Bloom

Layers

I see the layers of chains,
Breaking and crumbling off of you,
The more you grow in worship and adoration,
Of your Beloved Maker above.
The layers of strongholds,
Shall be uprooted out of your heart and mind.
You are released into the abundance of freedom,
And created flourish to become all you've been
destined to be,
Fearlessly and boldly,
Continually praising Him at the throne.

- Devona Fayana

Resurrection

Defeat had a tight grip from the very roots of your heart,
But through the redemption of His blood,
Resurrection and transformation became your portion.
And the restoration of your life,
Flourished and blossomed,
And healed every broken piece of your heart,
through the abundance of His grace.

- Devona Fayana

Lovely Grace

In His grace He resurrects your heart with the strength of His love.
You are renewed from death to life when your heart acknowledged Him as your Lord and Saviour, and through the power of the Holy Spirit you will flourish in your faith each day.

You will no longer look behind you, for you have a bright, flourishing future ahead of you.
Restoration is yours, found in the abundance of His mercy and unfailing love over your life.
Rest in the peace of His presence and trust His plan and timing for your life.

- Devona Fayana

Blossom Unfolding

The hardened shell that life has encrusted over your heart,
Shall now be transformed into wholeness and healing.
Let go of your past experiences and begin to unfold,
Openly beautifully and fearlessly,
Into the bright, blossoming flower you have been destined to become.
No longer will you be fearful,
Nor shall you be hidden,
Shying away from light that you are destined to remain.
Rise into your ordained sweet season of thriving and flourishing,
And immerse yourself into the fountain of life
In the fullness of His truly unfailing love.

- Devona Fayana

The Flowers Before They Bloom

Blossom Fearlessly

I want you to blossom fearlessly, flourishing confidently in the abundance of His love. May you be empowered and strengthened to believe again, to arise higher in your faith and be equipped and fed with His Word, that you may grow in the anointing and fulfil your wonderful calling in life with a spirit of excellence upon you.

As you bloom brighter in your confidence and firmly secure in your identity within Him, let your light shine before the world to see the radiance of Christ dwelling within you. That you may be a blessing to others and glorify your Beloved Father in heaven.

- Devona Fayana

Immersion

Immerse yourself entirely in His unfailing love.
Allow your heart to trust in wholeness and faith,
That you may dive in and dive deeply,
In His glorious fountain of life.
Entirely and fearlessly, without the doubts of holding back.
For in His presence is a place of restoration and refuge,
The wonderful abundance of His peace,
Satisfies every ounce of empty space of your heart.
Be overflowing with His peace, and may your joy be full.

- Devona Fayana

Let Go and Fall Deep

Let your heart go of everything concerning all that was behind you, detach yourself from the past and may every worry within your present circumstances be demolished as you immerse yourself in His arms.

Embrace the fullness of His love like you've never experienced before and your heart will enter into a whole new season of healing and new beginnings.

Be transformed through the renewing of your mind, by meditating on His Word whilst you dwell underneath the shadow of the almighty.

- Devona Fayana

New Creation

Your ways are not His ways,
Nor are your thoughts His thoughts,
Through which as you lovingly surrender your heart to His,
He will beautifully nourish and renew all through you,
Right from the roots of your spirit to the depths of your heart,
New seasons and revival shall blossom,
wonderfully through.

- Devona Fayana

The Flowers Before They Bloom

Trust His Ways

God's way of thinking is completely different to our way of thinking. He is El Shaddai, God almighty.
The beautiful one who is truly sovereign and different compared to us, through which our hearts must entrust Him with every area and situation concerning our lives.
The Lord is the beginning and the end, He sees the full timeline of your life. I encourage you to give your worries and concerns to the Lord, for He will deal with it and provide all of your needs.

God is not a Father who seems afar off, He is always near and ready to help you. God is love and there is nobody on this earth will ever be able to compare with Him. Through His grace you have become a new creation, and every single day of your life the Lord is faithful to continue to do a good work within your heart. Whatever you need, give it to the Lord in prayer. For He is able and willing to take good care of you.

- Devona Fayana

The Pruning

He cuts through the hidden parts of your heart,
And prunes every part of your spirit and soul,
That you may be fruitful in all things,
Flourishing in graceful character and
transformation of your thoughts.
So that you will bloom in and through,
Whatever situations that you may face,
For you will not be moved,
Regardless of the circumstances,
Because God is within you,
You will not fall.

- Devona Fayana

The Refining

Pruning is never a pleasant process to experience. But it's one of the most important experiences one could ever face. God is like a potter moulding the clay, we are like the clay being moulded on the potters wheel. Within us all, there are many imperfections. All have fallen short of the glory of God. And it is the Lord who is refining and transforming you each day to grow and blossom in wholeness and fruitfulness.

Refrain from feeling discouraged of the process that you are going through, because during every moment God is faithful to hold you, embrace you and use every situation for His glory and for good. Whenever you feel uncomfortable, discouraged and dismayed, run into the presence of your Saviour in worship and in prayer. Remembering to come to Him with thanksgiving, but always remembering you can come to your Heavenly Father for help and encouragement on any situation for He truly cares about you.

- Devona Fayana

Song of Deliverance

May you find freedom singing in the storm,
And dancing with resilience upon disappointment.
Let not your thoughts and emotions dictate,
The realities of truth.
The truth of His Word.
That forever holds you grounded and keeps you anchored,
And fully armoured in the beauty of His love.

- Devona Fayana

Sing Your Heart Out

There is freedom in worship, and deliverance within praise. In the difficult seasons of my life the Lord revealed to me that worship is what helps us go through the storm in victory. That we may take our focus off our problems and circumstances, and carry our attention onto the goodness of the Lord to bring Him glory and to meditate on His beautiful Word.

Chains break and darkness flees in the midst of worship, for you begin to immerse yourself in the presence of the Lord with a heart of gratitude, radiating fruitfulness. As you cultivate your love for worship regardless of the circumstances you find yourself in, you will not be moved. For God is with you throughout all seasons and no weapon formed against you will be able to prosper. Because you serve a God who is loving, faithful, wonderful and true. He is able to deliver you, keep you safe and transform you into the best version of yourself as you walk in the fullness of abundance of joy within the gift of life.
 - Devona Fayana

Let Go and Look On

Let go of what was,
Look on to what is to come.
Remind yourself of His wonderful promises each day,
And pursue the beauty of His heart,
As you find change and transformation in His presence.

- Devona Fayana

In His Love

In His love, there is joy. In His love there is security. In His love there is provision and protection. Grow and blossom within the love of your Beloved, for He will not disappoint you. I know that many of us have come from various experiences of life where we have been hurt and there may be too much emotions of fear or disappointment to even believe for positivity within the future. But when you are so immersed and enwrapped within the glorious arms and presence of the Lord, you are safe and secure in His arms.

God is a good Heavenly Father who will ensure that you are taken care of, because He only wants the best for you. He only wants you to be blessed, increased and fully well provided for. Refrain from yielding into fear dear one, and trust in the Lord's promises and His love towards you. For His love is unfailing and wonderfully true.

- Devona Fayana

Incorruptible

Let not your heart be troubled,
The ways of your past do not define you.
Neither be dismayed on the things that are behind you,
For Christ has come to purify, beautify and sanctify you,
Through His precious, incorruptible blood,
That you will look ahead to your wonderful promise,
Of the eternal, wonderful, abundant life,
That He has made available to you.

- Devona Fayana

Be Intentional With Your Surroundings

I encourage you to guard your heart and be intentional with who you surround yourself with. I truly believe that as you grow closer to the Lord and blossom beautifully within your spirit, you can sometimes be reminded of who you was or what you have done in your past. But I want to let you know that it's not what is behind you that defines you, it's the Lord who validates you wonderfully and gracefully in His love that is not comprehendible.

That's the beautiful thing I adore about the gospel and His heart towards us, regardless of what we have been through, He has clothed us with beauty and purified us in His grace. All He asks is that we love Him with all our hearts, minds and soul as we love others too. May we put Him first in all that we do, and never allow anyone to hold you back.

- Devona Fayana

Forgive Yourself

In your season of spring,
I urge you to forgive yourself.
Refrain from beating yourself up,
For the things you used to do,
And the person you used to be,
Because true freedom takes place.
When you realise the beauty of the gospel,
And the reality of what the Lord has done for you.
Learn to forgive and see yourself in love,
For you are forgiven, truly adored and valued,
In the eyes of the Almighty God.

- Devona Fayana

Forgive

Dear one, forgive yourself. For God has forgiven you and Christ has won the victory.
Never allow the accuser to hold you back to be hindered to your past, because there is so much beautiful things ahead of you that the Lord wants to spring forth. Your future is bright, and your life is full of light. May your light radiate beautifully to others and be an inspiration and blessing to all those who come near.

- Devona Fayana

Forgiven

The creator of the universe is in love with you,
He adores you from the fullness of His heart.
He loves you with an everlasting love to forgive you of your sins,
And to water you with His Word.
That through His grace, you may flourish and increase in all things.
When guilt and shame arises,
Know and remember whom it is you belong to,
And who's blood from which you have been redeemed.

- Devona Fayana

Never Separated From Love

There is nothing that you've done that can ever separate you from His love. His love is not comprehendible, so far above our own understanding. Fall deeply into His love, never look back and press on forward into His presence through worship and intimate time within prayer.

- Devona Fayana

Stay Anchored

Ensure to stay anchored in the truth,
Through remaining rooted in the security of His Word.
So that in the fire you will not be moved,
For He has promised you, that the fire will not burn you.
Nor the storms will be able overwhelm you.
Remain and abide in Him,
As you dwell underneath the shadow of the Almighty.

- Devona Fayana

Emotions vs Truth

When your emotions are running high and your strength feels low. May the word of God empower you and find security by not what you feel, but the truth of what you know.
You know the Lord's word is incorruptible and holds mighty powder over your life, so begin to declare His word always. That your mind shall be renewed, strengthened and realigned with the beauty and goodness of His truth.

- Devona Fayana

Beautiful Beginnings

May your time for beautiful beginnings,
beautifully arise,
Let those people and those thoughts who grip you back,
Be completely let go,
And find yourself gracefully and fervently back on track.

- Devona Fayana

Beauty and Goodness

Begin to live your life within expectancy of good news and positivity each day. For the Lord is able and willing to bless you, that you may grow in joy because He wants you to enjoy the gift of life that He has given you.

Radiate your heart of gratitude and raise up praises to the Lord for He is good and a wonderful provider. Lift your head and begin to feel excited again, for the better days are blossoming forward in your life.

- Devona Fayana

Discipline of Mind

Keep a close eye on the details,
And the roots of your thoughts.
Train your mind to think positively and in accordance with His Word.
For as you remain disciplined, entirely in the beauty of revelation of Him,
You will flourish and blossom,
With fruitfulness manifesting in every way,
And throughout all the areas of your precious, cherished life.

- Devona Fayana

Healing Hearts

As you transition in dear seasons,
He will heal the hardened areas of your hearts,
And replace your heart of stone,
Into a heart of flesh,
That you may love and forgive, fearlessly again.
Forgive those who mistreated you,
That you may also be forgiven,
And find the fullness of freedom,
Manifesting gloriously in your soul.

- Devona Fayana

Budding

Behold, I am doing a new thing; now it springs forth, do you not perceive it?
I will make a way in the wilderness and rivers in the desert. - Isaiah 43:19

The Flowers Before They Bloom

By His wonderful grace, you have made it through the stormy seasons. The Lord in His faithful love has uprooted everything within you that ever withheld you from flourishing forward. The tough times of pruning has gradually faded as your petals have began to bud and appear beautifully.
The budding season of our lives within our walk with God is when you have entered into a time of healing, deliverance and refreshment. The hard work of pruning, discipline and persistent prayer has helped you, for now you are beginning to be bud forth and glisten with excitement, peace, clarity and joy as the Lord is about to prosper you into your blossoming season.

As you begin to bud, you are transitioning from the old you into the new you! There will be beautiful new beginnings, new ways, new levels of potency and strength within the fruits of the Spirit cultivating stronger and stronger from within you! You are His beloved daughter, flourishing underneath the shade of the Almighty. This is one of the most crucial seasons for you to remain spiritually disciplined as your align your mind with His wonderful word.

The Flowers Before They Bloom

I want to encourage you to nurture yourself well from now on. I am not necessarily speaking about nurturing our outer beauty, but ensuring that we are nourishing ourselves well spiritually.

In order to become the woman God has called you to be, as well as experiencing the fullness of all the abundant blessings that He has for you, one of the most beautiful and important things to do in the budding season is to feed on His Word and He will blossom you. The Word of God provides us with spiritual nutrition which enables our minds and our hearts to come into alignment with God's will. Through meditating on His Word, we are able to grow to become fruitful and prosperous in all that we do. His Word guides us into peace and truth. Not only that, but I also want to encourage you to immerse yourself in His presence. Spend time with Him! Fall deeper and deeper in love with Him more and more each day. Experiment with various ways on how you can spend time with the Lord.
I can assure you, that all the healings, miracles, transformation and answers are found in Him! He has everything that you need. Rest still in His presence.

Flourishing In Fortress

Let your heart rest in the stillness of His presence,
He will cover you with His feathers,
The showers of His true love will nurture and restore your soul.
And under His wings you will take refuge,
As you are planted in the mighty hands of your fortress,
He will bud and blossom you,
And you will become more beautiful than you have ever been before.

- Devona Fayana

Sweet Faithfulness

With the thick presence of magnificent glory
hovering over you,
His radiant love outshines the darkest places of
your heart.
Every desolate place of heartbreak and
brokenness,
Blooms peacefully and fruitfully,
Into beautiful testimonies of His faithfulness.
Resting sweetly, and firmly planted in His love.

- Devona Fayana

Beautiful Adoration of Glory

The magnitude of His unfailing love covers me,
like the radiant sunlight.
He is my everlasting light,
And my glorious salvation.
I will love and adore Him, all the days of my life.
His goodness and mercy pursues me,
The wonderful works of His hand adorns me,
with the fullness of His joy.
I am ever grateful being the apple of His eye,
Forever I will love Him.
Forever He will reign.

- Devona Fayana

The Flowers Before They Bloom

Weight of Love

The weight of His love embraced me with otherworldly strength.
His love folded inwards, into the depths of my thirsty and weakened soul.
Through His living water, my thirst was quenched.
For He resurrected the dead roots of my heart,
Every part that was abandoned and abused.
The outpouring of His lovely spirit overflowed within me,
And I felt Him touch deep within my soul,
When He declared into my Spirit, and said that I was His,
For I have never felt so wanted, with such strong weight of love.
Worth and value was found in through His grace and faithfulness,
Who knew until now,
Someone would have thought I was beautiful enough,
To be protected, adored and faithfully carried.

- Devona Fayana

Sweet Righteousness

Sweet words are like honeycomb,
Pleasant to the soul,
Health to the bones.
Resurrection to the heart,
Peace to the mind.
Through His Word, I believed
And by His stripes, I was healed.

- Devona Fayana

The Flowers Before They Bloom

Blossoming Song

The budding season has come,
For you to blossom in strength,
And sing your Maker, a new sweet song,
Of victory and joy,
With flourishing gratitude of His faithfulness.
For you have grown through the storm,
And made it this far to greatness,
Sing and worship beautiful one,
For you have endured,
And He showers you in His love.

- Devona Fayana

Light and Life

For so long I searched for the true meaning of life,
My heart broken, my soul empty,
Of the draining cares and anxieties of this world.
But one day I encountered a glorious light,
And that light was found in the Word,
The Word that was with God.
The Word that is God.
Through Him we were all created,
And in Him, the true source of life, the light and love,
Can only be found in Him.

- Devona Fayana

Love Light Peace

The love of my life,
Is the light of my heart.
He glistens so gloriously and exquisitely in my soul,
I am revived and resurrected through the power of His Spirit.
For the breath of life is indwelling softly within me,
His light has overcome every dark area of my entire being,
And has outshined and overflowed within me.
My light, my love and peace,
Is so pure and true.
He has lit up my life,
And has made all things new.

- Devona Fayana

Pleasant Songs

He sings pleasantly and wonderfully over you,
Encouraging you to blossom gracefully,
Keep on growing and glowing with His light,
Never feel overwhelmed with the anxieties of your surroundings,
For His song is nurturing your faith,
And awakening your very soul.
Pay no attention to the cares of this world,
Fix your mind on the beautiful realities of heaven,
The place from where you belong.
And He who dwells there, is the one who keeps you strengthened.

- Devona Fayana

The Flowers Before They Bloom

The Confident Bloom

Every flower is diverse,
Each petal has it's stunning uniqueness.
They bloom at their own pace,
When blossoming fruitfully, it's never a race,
Nor a competition, for one to compare itself to another,
The rose is not the sunflower.
Nor the peony, a tulip.
Each is clothed with beauty like no other,
And what's even more beautiful,
Is that their wonderful beauty compliments each other.

- Devona Fayana

Blooming Forward

As you are blooming,
Never look back,
To the place from where you came,
For your past doesn't dictate the wonderful future,
That God has divinely orchestrated for you.

- Devona Fayana

The Flowers Before They Bloom

Fruitful Harvest

I know it has felt like a never ending storm,
But the raindrops you feel,
Will cause a harvest of fruitfulness,
For there are no flowers without rain,
And no rainbow without a storm,
But through the aftermath of it all,
The sun shines gracefully and gloriously over you,
Arise in your strength,
And may your faith in God flourish.

- Devona Fayana

The Flowers Before They Bloom

Painting Imperfections

Refrain from the pressure of perfection,
Let go of the destructive narrative,
That all you must be,
And everything that you do,
Should be beautiful and faultless.
Sweet one, it is such an unrealistic idea for you to reach,
For there is only One who is perfect in all of His ways,
And in your weakness, His power is made perfect,
And through His blood, you are redeemed.
Refrain from striving for perfection,
He moulds you and blossoms you everyday,
So do not be discouraged,
And never be dismayed,
For He loves you no matter what,
Keep your roots clinging onto all of the promises that He has said.

- Devona Fayana

Abiding Bloom

Abide in His love,
As He abides gracefully in you,
When you rest and pursue obedience in His presence,
A wonderful multitude of fruit begins to flourish in the midst,
And from the sorrow of your tears.
Birth transformation within every part of your life,
Forever you'll remain secure in His love,
Forever His goodness and mercy will pursue you too.

- Devona Fayana

Field of Flowers

In a field of flowers,
Of many beautiful kinds,
There are multitudes upon multitudes of diversity,
Various designs and unique creations of artistry,
There is beauty so potent that resides in you,
For you are fearfully and wonderfully made,
There is no reason to compare yourself to another,
Because God loves you so dearly,
You are beautiful, and lovely in His sight.

- Devona Fayana

The Flowers Before They Bloom

Flourishing Free

Darling you are free,
Free to fly in wholeness and greatness,
Into the abundant life He destined for you,
You are entirely free,
To love and to flourish without chains nor the weight of hinderances,
You are free to receive,
The glorious unfailing love,
That He fills and overflows in you.

- Devona Fayana

The Flowers Before They Bloom

Rose

He resurrected,
He rose,
He raised in the fullness of His reign,
For He has defeated,
Every work of failure and darkness in your life,
And replaced it with His magnificent light.
May your heart resurrect,
In wholeness within the truth of His Word,
And rise in the excellence of His grace.
Blossom beautifully and wholly,
In His abundance love.

- Devona Fayana

Blossoming

I am a rose of Sharon, a lily of the valleys.
- Song of Solomon 2:1

The Flowers Before They Bloom

Beloved daughter of God, your time of blossoming has come. Be immersed in the Lord's arms as He embraces you with His wings. Take shelter and refuge in Him, for He covers you with your unfailing love.

As you experience the windows of heaven open up beautifully over your life, pouring out abundant joy and blessings, be sure to stay connected to the vine. Remain beautifully in intimacy with the Lord, for you will never ever stop flourishing. Always be open minded and led by His precious Holy Spirit. May doors of opportunities open up for you as the Lord blesses and increases you more and more each day.

As you continue to prosper, may the Lord be your priority always. May you pursue His heart and grow in the abundance of His overwhelming, glorious love.

When you begin to see your prayers come to pass as you walk in the wholeness and contentment that you've always admired, ensure that you remain submitted and surrendered to God.

The Flowers Before They Bloom

For through submission and surrender we remain humbled before the Lord. Never forget that He was there for you during your hardest moments. Walk in reverence and remembrance of God's wonderful faithfulness to you throughout every season of your life.

Radiate with gratitude and thankfulness each day, soak yourself in His presence through prayer and absorb yourself in His word.

There is nothing in this world that will fulfil you besides the Lord, your Beloved Redeemer Himself. I cannot express how much He adores you. His love for you is unlike any other in this world. Embrace your new beginnings and continue to worship the Lord for all the wonderful things He has done and is always doing in your life.

Beloved, It Is Time

Beloved this is your time to shine,
And blossom in beauty,
As you worship your true love,
Within spirit and in truth.
Believe whole heartedly that you truly belong to Him,
For you have transformed gracefully in transition,
And remained faithful in the process.
Now new things will spring forth,
This is the beginning of season,
For one of the most beautiful times of your life.

- Devona Fayana

Cherished Celebration

May your petals of confidence flourish and grow,
As you let go,
And let God take control,
Of everything that dwells within you,
Persist with your beautiful heart of gold,
encrusted with gratitude,
And your mouth full of thanksgiving,
For the Lord cherishes you,
And in due time, you will be celebrating and overflowing,
With the overwhelming joy of the Lord.
You shall sing and you shall dance,
As you walk in the fullness of your destiny,
And enjoy the fruit of your life,
That He has already, beautifully pre-planned.

- Devona Fayana

Blessed Dreams

What you've always dreamed of,
Is surely on the way.
Happily ever afters do exist,
As long as you keep Christ in the midst.
Through prayer and worship you will persist,
And enjoy the glorious fruit of your life in it's entirety.
For beautiful you are,
And gracious, the Lord is faithfully to you.
Your life is blessed by the wonderful hand of God Almighty.

- Devona Fayana

Seeds of Greatness

Expand your creativity and imagination,
As you pursue the lovely heart of the Lord,
For He has planted,
Beautiful things,
In the deepest places of your heart,
Seek and you will eventually find,
And wonderful doors of opportunity will open for you,
May you praise Him forever.

- Devona Fayana

Look To The Sky

Beautiful one,
You have come so far,
And blossomed so beautifully,
Rising in strength,
And flourishing within the favour of the Lord,
Look up to the stunning sky,
Reach out to the heavens,
And immerse yourself in the beauty of His presence.

 - Devona Fayana

The Flowers Before They Bloom

Heaven's Flower Garden

"Arise! Talitha Cumi!" He sung to me.
His voice is like a rush of many waters,
Sounding like a soft, sweet melody,
The season of refreshment and revival has come.
And His Word resurrected me,
So I rose in the strength of His Spirit
Gracefully rejoicing in His mercy.
I am blooming like a sunflower, resting
underneath the warmth of the Son,
And soaking in the waves of heat within His
radiant love.
His Word waters my soul and nurtures me all day
long,
I am revived by His living water,
Through Him, I am made alive.
My Spirit is whole, found dwelling firmly planted,
In the palms of His wonderful hands.

- Devona Fayana

In His Hands

You are like a rose in His hands,
Skilfully created and beautifully designed,
Blossoming in the midst of fruitfulness,
Whilst being securely planted in Him.
You rest in tranquility underneath His protection and shade,
Sitting exquisitely and beautifully, absorbing His lovely presence.
He watches over you with awe, because of your beauty,
He is pleased of the stunning work which He has created,
Bloom in the confidence, concerning your identity in Him.

- Devona Fayana

The Flowers Before They Bloom

Joy

The tears that you cried,
Were rooted from strength and not in weakness,
They are part of the significance,
Of your beautiful process,
And blossoming into glorious transformation.
Your tears of sorrow have been transformed,
To be replaced with tears of joy,
Fall in love with rejoicing,
For this is the season where joy will overflow more in your life,
Now like never before.

- Devona Fayana

Flask Of Oil

I pour out before you,
Everything I am and everything I have,
Because you are worthy,
So wonderful and true,
You've sanctified my soul,
And you, my dearly beloved,
Have made everything new.

- Devona Fayana

Beauty In The Process

Beloved He has won,
The wonderful victory for you,
That you may be entirely free,
So you may no longer be blind,
But for you to flourish in your faith and clearly see.
The glory and beauty of the Lord,
Blossoming within intimacy with Him,
For there is beauty in the process,
And rest peacefully in grace,
And eternity in love,
And being perfectly loved by Him.

- Devona Fayana

Letters In Bloom

Rise Up Beautiful

Beloved Daughter of God,

I want to fill your heart with warmth and encouragement to know that you are a beautiful, anointed, chosen, loved and gifted woman of God. That whatever the enemy meant to use to harm you, God will turn it around for your good. I want you to arise from where you are and stand in confidence, with the beautiful security to know your identity, value and worth is found in Christ.

Awake from your slumber and remove your old garments of disappointment and shame, for God has crowned you with grace, wonderful love and splendour. Never compare yourself to another woman, for God has created us all differently, the best way that He pleases. A rose blossoms and never compares itself to a sunflower or a peony. Yet they are all absolutely stunning and beautifully crafted by the hands of God.

The Flowers Before They Bloom

Therefore neither should you compare yourself to another. Embrace all of who God has called you to be, grow in confidence and boldness. Let your heart soak in all of His love and feel the warmth of His arms over you. Wherever you go, He goes. Because He has promised to be with you always.

Take some time aside, rest in the presence of the Lord and ask Him to reveal to you the beautiful things about you. If you have any ideas that you've also come up with, write them down. Speak them out loud and let it really absorb into your mind and spirit. All the wonderful, positive aspects of you. For you are truly loved and valued by God. He has blessed you with many gifts, talents, passions, assignments and wonderful plans for your future. Begin to get excited again about the lovely life that God has planned for you!

No Rain, No Flowers

Dear Daughter of God,

Many times the most beautiful things take time and things must also go through a process. I am truly in awe of flowers and the journey that God takes them through. Then I came to realise that the more I look into flowers and how they are formed and flourished, I see that we too are not too different from them. Both you and I are similar to flowers more than you think.

I see it as when we give our lives to Christ, He plants us in His hands and deeper into the depths of His love. However during the growth process it can feel uncomfortable when He prunes us. There may be parts within our character, our mindsets and even things or people in our lives that He desires to cut off in order that we may blossom forward and bear fruit.

The Flowers Before They Bloom

To be really honest with you, there are so many factors and things that we are surrounded in within our lives that can cause us to be hindered in our growth process, and that's the beauty of pruning. I know it may be difficult and it certainly isn't easy to let go of certain things that we've held on to in life, but we know that God knows best. For He knows us better than we know ourselves.

What do you believe God is leading you to let go of? Are there any areas in your life where you just know and believe that it's time to move on? Give it to the Lord in prayer and He will lead you in the way you ought to go.

I also see ourselves in flowers in terms of the importance of being nurtured through watering and nourishing ourselves with the Word of God in order that we may grow. Beautiful things do not grow when they are malnourished. The more we saturate ourselves in worship, in prayer and in study time with the Lord, the more we will flourish and blossom to become more fruitful to be pleasing to Him and a blessing to others.

The Flowers Before They Bloom

I encourage you, that if you have been through a stormy season do not worry. God will use what you've been through for the advancement of His glory and to mould and shape you to become the stronger, resilient, beautiful person who is securely planted in His hands.
You are being transformed and blossomed to be a person who is confident in their identity and position within Christ, to grow in confidence of His word and His truth concerning His love for you. Trials may come, but it can only make you flourish to be more fruitful and beautiful as you help others with the lessons you have learnt also.

Never be discouraged regardless of what seasons you have faced, for God has promised that He is always with you, and no weapon formed against you will be able to prosper. He will take care of you always, for you are always in His heart.

The Flowers Before They Bloom

Hopes and Dreams

Sweet Daughter of God,

I know you may have hopes and dreams where your life is filled with the glorious fruit of abundance and joy. Where all your prayers have finally been answered and you're walking in the best seasons of your life. I can assure you, that as long as you are walking with God, then better days will always be truly ahead of you. God knows every desire of your heart and He has heard your prayers. However I also know that if someone has lived a life of heartache and trials, hope sometimes may be lost. You begin to wonder if this is it, and what does life have in store for you. I want to encourage you that as you place your heart and trust in the Lord, the days that are before you will not be like the past disappointments that you have faced.

The Flowers Before They Bloom

When God created you, He had so much planned. Many things are in store for you. Beautiful things for you to do, achieve and blossom into, as your heart grows closer and closer to Him.

Life was created to have a lovingly, deep relationship with God and experience the fullness of every joyful plan of His for our lives.

God desires for you to be happy and completely joyful regardless of circumstances because you belong to Him, secured in His unfailing love as His sweet child. As your Father, Lover, Saviour and Friend, He wants to be in control of your life, for He knows what is best, and He knows the steps you ought to take in oder to be the most fruitful and joyful person you can be.

God does not want you to experience sadness, disappointment, hurt, heartbreak or anger. He wants to wrap you up in His love and continue to shower you with His glorious grace. God wants to continually be your provider, your protecter. Be the source of all of your needs.

The Flowers Before They Bloom

Take a moment to reflect by sitting still in His presence and soaking up His love for you. Remember and hold it close in your heart that He is the lover and redeemer of your soul. He wants you. You are loved, adored and chosen. To live a life beautifully orchestrated by Him. Hold on close to His heart, for He will never let go of yours.

Disciplining Your Thoughts

Daughter of the King,

The Lord has created our minds in such a powerful way. That's why it's so imperative that our minds are daily renewed by the beauty of His word on a regular, consistent basis. His word is truth and His word is also light. Without the light constantly filling our minds its so easy for darkness to creep through if you're not disciplined. And I honestly do believe that sometimes thoughts of darkness rooted from our emotions may seem so small, such as doubting an area that you're believing in God for or even saying something negative over yourself. But it has the power to shift the direction your life is going.

It is something I have struggled with for a while, but God took me through a season of spiritual discipline that my mind may come into true alignment with the truth, power and authority found in His divine word.

The Flowers Before They Bloom

What are you believing in God for? There may be things that you have been waiting on for quite some time, but there are moments that you may have faced where doubt begins to invite itself into your thoughts and it begins to break down the faith that you have built up. You could also be possibly struggling with your self esteem but your thoughts have been quite negative concerning areas of your life that make you feel quite upset.

There are plenty of subtle ways where our emotions have an effect on our thoughts, through which our thoughts may begin to create a pattern in how we think which will have a knock on effect on not only how we perceive ourselves but also how we see the world and everything else in general.

The most effective step we take in times such as this is to clothe ourselves with the full armour of God. It is our spiritual armour that will keep us protected and equipped to stand firm and not be utterly destroyed by any attacks of the enemy.

The Flowers Before They Bloom

For many years I had battled with negative thinking, I began to see the negative thinking actually having an effect on my life and I came to a point where I had enough! I took up my armour, as well as placing on a garment of praise and gratitude daily, and this is where I began to see glorious shifts happening in my life taking place.

Whenever you think of a negative thought or something that may discourage you, come against it with a scripture that shuts down those thoughts completely. For God's word is truth and it's also known as a double edged sword, use your weapons to cut off and destroy any destructive thought patterns in your life.

Do not believe the lie that you are not good enough, that you are not loved, that you will never get married, that you won't succeed. We come against it with the powerful word of God. Therefore I encourage you, if you haven't already, begin to meditate on the scriptures and let it saturate every part of your mind and heart.

The Flowers Before They Bloom

Receive healing and restoration within yourself into a state of wholeness, joy and gratitude through the help of the Holy Spirit.
Whatever is lovely, whatever is right, whatever is honourable, dwell on these things. Surround yourself with peace, love and joy always.
Discipline your mind to be thankful and hopeful, filled with faith in every circumstance and in due time, you'll see transformation within every area of your life bloom through. Because I truly do believe, that is all starts from the mind.

Hearts Change

Beautiful Daughter of God,

I am in love with how magnificently wonderful the Lord is in His faithfulness, I admire His loving and unchanging heart. I adore His faithfulness towards us. Because the world we dwell in is truly filled with sorrow and times of difficulties, it is inevitable that as life goes by our hearts may have gone through a season of brokenness or disappointment. But the Lord is good, and He is faithful. He is not one to give up on anyone, especially one that has a willing heart to be healed, shaped and moulded within His hands.

His words are promising and true, we can rest assured that He will never leave or forsake us. In His grace we have become a new creation in Christ Jesus. We are as clay being transformed in the hands of the almighty, being shaped into the beautiful person that He desires for us to be.

The Flowers Before They Bloom

In seasons of divine transformation, our hearts must be open to the leading of His precious Holy Spirit, that we may yield to Him and His will in order for His purposes to not only be established in our lives, but in our hearts.

Something I am coming to learn to understand is that in order to truly be fruitful, or even walk in the fullness of God's glorious promises for us, we have to be transformed from the inside that the fruit within us may radiate outwardly. We blossom within our inner beauty and cultivate the fruits of the Spirit through the renewing of our minds. I believe that the renewing of our minds can be accomplished through the power of God's word and spending time with Him. In your season of change and trusting God to fulfil what He promised to you, nurture yourself with Him Word as He showers you with His love within His wonderful presence.

May you be saturated with His word and grow in knowledge of Him more and more each day.

There Is Hope In Your Future

Dear Daughter of God,

There comes a point in your life where in order to move forward, you have to refuse looking back on the things that were behind you. I have battled with this area where I truly found it difficult to press on forward to the goal and the beautiful promises that God has given to my concerning my future. Sometimes I really do believe it's as though if we don't receive the true healing and closure from our past, the weight of our guilt, shame and disappointment can chain us back into thinking that we are not strengthened or equipped enough to move forward. But in moments such as these, the best thing we ought to do is grip onto the word and promises of God. That regardless of who we were or what we have done, His glorious incorruptible word is still standing firmly over your life.

The Flowers Before They Bloom

There is so much treasurable beauty and indescribable love found in God's grace. By His grace, He looks after us and have given us the gift of eternal life. Eternal life is available to all who place their belief in Jesus Christ. And through which, as you journey through beautiful intimacy and relationship with God, your life will cultivate into fruitfulness and abundance of joy. For this is His will concerning your life, to live it to the fullest, hand in hand with Him to bring glory and honour to His name. May hope and faith blossom in your heart, that you may grow in the belief that your life ahead of you shall be well and fruitful.

There are many individuals in the bible that had a difficult past. However God still got the glory out of their lives in the most wonderful ways. For example, Queen Esther. She was a young orphan and her past may have been filled with difficulties, loss and grief. On the other hand, the Lord still blessed and exalted her to royalty for His purposes. We can also think of Ruth, the beautiful moabite widow who moved to Bethlehem and married a noble man of God and eventually became the great grandmother of King David!

The Flowers Before They Bloom

There can be so many other remarkable stories that I can share with you, but it truly shows that God is able to do anything within the life of anyone! Regardless of your background or the mistakes that have been made. The Lord makes things beautiful in it's time, He is the master artist that can transform things from nothing into something so glorious. He is able to to wonderful things in your life, even the things you may think are impossible, He can do.

Dear one, there is always hope in your future whenever God is in the centre of your heart and life. Trust Him, for He is able. Nothing is impossible with God, and His tender mercies are new every morning. May you feel refreshed with a revival of hope every day you wake up, for God has wonderful plans for you.

The Flowers Before They Bloom

A Rose In His Hands

Beloved Daughter of God,

You are truly as a rose in His hands, firmly planted in His truth and lavished with His care. You have not been buried, rather you have been planted as you dwell underneath the warm love of the almighty. Refrain from being dismayed during the process of your growth, for time must run it's course as beautiful things prepare to take place. On your journey in relationship with God, the Lord takes you on a wonderful journey and blossoms you into the fullness of who He has called you to be. Though in order for something to grow, it needs the right things to flourish and sustain it.

May you blossom underneath the warmth of the Son, as His light glows from within you and radiates throughout your life. Whilst He showers you with His love and rains over you with His faithfulness, may you grow in knowledge of Him as you absorb every truth of His Word and let it remain in your heart.

The Flowers Before They Bloom

Cultivate your relationship with Him, and you will bloom in every area of life.

It's so important to nurture the roots of our hearts and not work on things that are on the surface. If we truly are believing for healing and transformation, our new beginnings and seasons will come as long as we take care of the roots of every place concerning our lives. The roots of your heart, being set free by letting go of what was behind you. The roots of your mind, walking in freedom and deliverance from strongholds that held you bound. Look right into the depth of your being and identify what exactly holds you back from prospering and flourishing on forwards in the fullness of who Christ wants you to be.

As you blossom in Christ, never be afraid to open up your heart to Him. Be open and honest with Him during every moment. Share every thought and every care with Him. Because He is your everlasting companion who is able to look after you and give you all that you possibly need in your life.

The Flowers Before They Bloom

Do not despise the day of small beginnings. You have been firmly planted within the arms of your beloved Saviour and secured eternally in His love.

Life Is Full of Surprises

Beautiful Woman of God,

As you walk throughout your life, hand in hand with God, may there be many pleasant surprises and miracles that come your way. I know you may have experienced the hurt of going through disappointment in your life over and over again. So much to the point where it is as though you find it difficult to believe in anything great coming forth into your life again. But I want to reassure you that the Lord has many wonderful surprises in store for you.

He knit you in your mothers womb for a purpose, you were not a mistake but a pleasant surprise on this earth. For you were ordained by God Himself. He has wonderful plans for you to give you a flourishing future and a great hope! It doesn't matter what your current situation looks like, believe in faith that God has better things in store for you.

The Flowers Before They Bloom

The bible mentions that He is able to provide exceedingly and abundantly more than you can ask for or imagine. I encourage you to increase your faith like never before. To rise above those feelings of disappointment, no longer looking back but making the decision to look forward with expectancy with the knowledge of God's grace, power and faithfulness. Knowing deeply in your heart that the Lord wants to build your faith and trust in Him that He is willing and able to bless you with the desires of your heart. Being confident in the Lord's love for you, that He truly cares about every area of your life and He wants to make things right. You just need to let Him in, through the increase of your faith and praising Him in advance for what He is about to do.

The beauty of the surprises and miracles of life is that God is truly faithful, He showers His love on all. But He also blesses us in order to testify and share His goodness with others, that His glory may be seen and the gospel to be spread. Refrain from falling into the false idea that the Lord doesn't care about you or that He has forgotten you. That is far from the truth.

The Flowers Before They Bloom

Maybe He is waiting for you to open up your heart and let Him in deeper like never before. This is the beauty of the gospel, that Christ has come that we are able to be reconciled to God and walk in relationship with Him. That through repentance and believing in Him, we may live a life of abundance, fruitfulness and hope.

Pursue His heart, as He pursues yours. Ask Him to reveal His will within every season, remain obedient to Him always and then sooner than you know, your life will never be the same as you cultivate your relationship with Him.

The Flowers Before They Bloom

The Time of Your Restoration Has Come

Dear Daughter of The King,

The time of your restoration has come! I need you to let go of all that was behind you and for you to arise now with all the strength that is within you. Not only that, but also depending on His Spirit to strengthen you in your weakest moments. For you are no longer who you were before, and your past experiences or present hardships do not determine who you are either. You are fully redeemed, loved, cared for and well looked after by God Himself. There is nothing you can do to stop Him from caring about you. For there is no height nor depth that can separate you from Him glorious love concerning you.

In His love there is life. And within that life you will find restoration again. Restoration time has come for you to be restored of all that you have lost in your life. Your confidence, your strength, your dreams, your hopes, your faith, your finances, your career.

The Flowers Before They Bloom

It can be absolutely anything, whatever it is, God has the power to restore it. And He will restore it mightily within His sovereign power and strength. You are not defeated nor defined by the tough parts of your life, for you have been marked with His grace and covered by His precious blood.

Everything that seems dried up and weary in your life shall spring forth into fruitfulness, into alignment with His will for your life as you are resurrected as a new creation in Christ Jesus our Lord.

He clothes you with beauty, and lavishes you with His glorious grace. Never look down on yourself, for you are glowing with His light and covered with His unfailing love. The season of rain has passed away and now it is time for you to experience the spring season of blooming forth and bearing good fruit in every area and every way of your life, for His glory. For He is good and He loves you more than you could ever truly understand.

The Flowers Before They Bloom

Lift your head up high, child of God. Because the Lord has truly redeemed you. You are declared free and whole in His hands. And He will never, ever let you go. You are His. Rest in the Love of your Beloved Saviour.

Blooming In Every Season

Beautiful Daughter of God,

There is so much beauty found in the heart of Christ. He is the definition of love Himself, He is love and His love is like no other. True love heals every hurt and broken place in your soul. The love of Christ gathers together the shattered pieces of your heart and mends them together in wholeness with His care. The true love of the Lord does not multiply the sorrow and anxiety that you face, rather it takes it away if you open up your heart to Him and allow Him. He will dig so deeply into your mind, your heart, your soul and remove every feeling of worry and weariness.

A scripture that I resonate with so much is Isaiah 61:3, it mentions 'the garment of praise for the spirit of heaviness'.
During my life before I gave my heart to the Lord I was so weighed down with heaviness and the things of this world.

The Flowers Before They Bloom

But when I truly came to grow in revelation of the beauty of the love of the Lord, my heart opened up to Him. As I received His Word and believed in His truth, I blossomed with the garment of praise all over me. The heaviness fled away and He lifted off the burdens of this world.

Beautiful things take time, and there is a process that must go forward when great things are about to take place. So if you are also on the journey of finding healing and wholeness, take it easy and never be too hard on yourself. Rest in His love.

Be still and know that He is God. He is God who watches over your heart and is faithful to heal and restore all that has been damaged and hurt. He is your healer and the true lover of your soul. Continue to fall deeply in love, faith and trust in Him because He is so worthy and also able to provide exceedingly and abundantly for you in every way possible. Others may have failed you, but it is impossible for God to ever fail you. He never changes, He will love you today, tomorrow and always. Remain rooted and established in His love.

You Are Firmly Planted

Sweet Daughter of God,

I have much experience and gained wisdom of those seasons where you feel as though you have been buried in the dirt, forgotten about and gone through those darkest moments of abandonment, loss, loneliness and isolation. Those pivotal times of life where it seems like there is nobody around you that truly understands you and can comfort you the way you need so deeply.

Just like a seed in the soil, it may feel as though you have been buried but in actual truth you have been firmly planted. Taken care of by your Creator and the lover of your soul. Sometimes it feels as though nobody is there to shield you and hold you close during the windy storms, but God is always there with you. Even though you cannot see Him, He is always present. Especially close within in the times of need.

The Flowers Before They Bloom

There is great comfort in growing in intimacy with God in these hard, life changing moments. I believe the toughest times in life magnifies the truth that nobody is perfect and no-one can truly be your hero. Family and our circle of friends are truly a blessing, but there are times in our lives where our hearts are pouring out and crying for help, peace and comfort in the early hours at 3am whilst you are battling with the uncomfortable trials and seasons that you are facing.
I have been there.

There are times where I had to accept that my loved ones are honestly only human themselves, it's almost impossible to rely on another human being to be there 24/7. There came a time where I reached my breaking point in life and I began to cry out to God. The God who is omnipresent, omnipotent and omniscient. The God who knew my beginning and end, my secrets, my past, my deepest thoughts and all of my seasons. He who is present everywhere and has the power to fill me up with hope and strength. I wanted to rely on someone. I wanted a heart to run to where I felt overwhelmed with the drowning emotions in the late hours of the night.

The Flowers Before They Bloom

I needed a Saviour to run to and keep me safe and sound no matter what the reason or hour was. I turned to the loving, almighty God who never sleeps nor slumbers. The true, most loving God who is full of mercy and lovingkindness. I needed someone. I needed Him.

I believe that in seasons of planting, we are positioned in such places for a reason. The experience of loneliness is never easy, but sometimes you may be loved so much by God that He may place you in uncomfortable circumstances in order for you to reach out to Him intimately. He will not force you to want to get to know Him, but He may allow situations in your life to take place so that you may know Him as your Redeemer, Saviour and true lover of your soul unlike anyone else in your life.
Therefore I encourage you to not underestimate these lonely seasons of your life, instead press into God. Meet Him. Greet Him in like you never have before. Because truly I tell you from the depths of my heart, nothing else will be able to support, comfort and love us like He can eternally.

You Are Beautifully Clothed In Grace

Daughter of the King,

During the most difficult times of experiencing hardship, failure and disappointment it can be so easy to fall into the trap of feeling defeated and eventually wanting to let go and give up to become discouraged. I cannot express the amount of times I have felt this way.

Something I've had to learn is that the mistakes and disappointments that we may face do not define us. I believe that many of us have believed the lie that we are defined by the things that we have done. We are not defined by the external things, but the things internally. What defines us is what God says about us. Our heart's posture, our character and our relationship with God is much more valuable and important than what we can physically see in our lives.

The Flowers Before They Bloom

For many years I used to label myself as a failure or a disappointment due to the events that took place in my life, but when I discovered God's Word about me, my thoughts towards myself blossomed and transformed into something so positively beautiful that I have never experienced before. I began to align myself with His word.

I want to encourage you to never be too afraid to continue to press forward even when you do not understand. When it seems as though all hell is breaking loose and you cannot seem to see beyond what's currently happening in your life, may you arise and begin to walk by faith and not by sight. There is more to what you see now, and there is more to you than you know. The grace of God covers you and keeps you going day by day. By His loving grace, both you and I are able to stand with the beauty of resilience and strength.

Whilst you say no to fear, and whilst you shut the door to the feelings of defeat and failure, remind yourself that your feelings doesn't exactly equate to truth.

The Flowers Before They Bloom

Keep the truth of God's promises hidden safely deep within you and do not allow your heart's emotions to throw you off the promises of God.

There is usually a plan and a process to many good things that take place and flourish in one's life. Whether it's the promise of a more joyful seasons of life, a career, a life partner, financial matters, or friends.. you name it. Many of the things that we hope for do not happen instantly. My mom often tells me that Rome wasn't built in a day, and the beautiful promises and good plans that you are looking forward to often requires a process to take place.
Surely there may be ups and downs throughout seasons of life, however these situations enable ourselves to be strengthened and matured.

Refrain from allowing troubling seasons of your life to make you feel defeated, but see this as an opportunity to blossom in beauty and flourish in unwavering faith. The Lord's grace is sufficient for you and His strength will be made perfect in your times of weakness.

The Flowers Before They Bloom

In truth, I can honestly say that in my most vulnerable times of weakness, I have seen God's strength be magnified so potently. It's never a nice thing to experience hardships, but when I came to the realisation of how powerful, strong and wonderful the Lord is I was absolutely blown away by His grace and hand upon my life. I have seen Him move faithfully over the lives of others and He surely does the same for you too.
Do not be discouraged, because your life is dearly cherished by God. There are hard seasons and times that we may face in our lives but what's more important is that we know that the times are temporary and God holds us close firmly through the midst of it all.

The Flowers Before They Bloom

He Loves You Today, Tomorrow and Forevermore

Daughter of God,

As a good Father loves his children, so does your Heavenly Father exceed that in the love that He has towards you. His love towards you is unfailing and unmatchable. It doesn't matter what state your relationship is like with God, He loves you more than anyone else in existence. For He knows you better than anyone else, He especially knows you better than you even claim to know yourself. For He foreknew you before the foundation of the world, He knew you before He knit you beautifully in your mother's womb. Nothing can compare to the purest love of God. I know what it is to be alone, and I know what it is to feel unloved. When you look all around you and see many people but still feel lonely and isolated. When you're tired of mediocrity in your relationships and begin to crave the true intimacy. I have felt it.

The Flowers Before They Bloom

Every craving feeling for love and intimacy I have felt so deeply, but I have only found that in the heart of my Saviour. My thirst for love was never satisfied until I immersed myself in Him. I often find that people crave love and seek to find it in the wrong places, these things only quench our thirst for a moment, but eventually we thirst again and again. It is the love of God, and the outpouring of His unfailing love that satisfies that thirst eternally. Those who receive Him in such ways will never thirst again. He fulfils our every need and I'm so grateful for Him.

I believe that sometimes we come across feelings of guilt and shame when it comes to thinking that God has even loved us at our darkest, but there is nothing to feel guilty or ashamed about as long as we come clean, naked and bare before God. Repenting of all the things we've ever done wrong and allowing Him to heal and restore us like never before. It is when we strip ourselves before the Lord that we experience the wonderful power and revival of His glorious love and strength.

The Flowers Before They Bloom

Never feel like you have to hide things from Him, because God is actually already aware of everything you have experienced. What you previously done and what you have gone through has not changed the way He loves you. Invite Him into your heart, allow Him to come and flood your mind with the overflowing never ending peace and joy to sustain you.

Whether you may have known it or not, He has always been the anchor of your soul. His hand is always upon you. As His beloved creation and precious one, His love for you is unchanging. As you long for love, God longs for you. You will find satisfaction when you surrender your heart to the lover of your soul and invite Him in.

Immerse yourself in the truth of His Word and what He says about you. God says that you are fearfully and wonderfully made (psalm 139:14), God says that He has many good thoughts towards you, greater than the number of sand grains (psalm 139:14), God says that He loves you so much that He gave His only Son for you (john 3:16).

The Flowers Before They Bloom

I know sometimes we desire other forms of love, whether its a partner or to have more friends, or even to have a restored relationship with a family member. However as I mentioned earlier, nothing and nobody can compare to the glorious love of God for you. Until you open up your heart to Him, satisfaction in love cannot be found in anything else. Who could truly love with the most purest and powerful love there is? Only the creator and definition of love Himself. He is love. God is love. Love is God. He is all that you are searching for.

The Flowers Before They Bloom

You Are Loved and Fully Known

Beautiful Daughter of The King,

In this wonderful wide world filled with many people, who knew it could be easy to feel so unloved and lonely at times? We are currently living in a generation where many of us are striving to be loved and validated through seeking attention on social media, some of us often validate what we see. But the beauty of true love rooted in God reveals to us that we do not always have to rely on the things we see, nor how we feel. But to place our trust in the truth of God's Word.

For many years I had struggled with my identity, it became a problem for me to learn how to love myself and see the beautiful positive sides to me. I think deep down it was because I looked to others to love and accept me in order to love myself. What a tragedy it is to turn to everyone and everything else but Jesus. I never truly understood what true love was until I encountered Him.

The Flowers Before They Bloom

All these years before I met the Lord I thought that love was a feeling, not a choice. I believe that real love is surely a choice and not just a feeling that comes and goes that is easily shaken by circumstances. Through which, previously I used to try and keep up an image to impress others in order to love me and to make me feel better. I also truly did believe that I was not good enough to be loved by God. I thought that the requirements for God to love you was for you to be a perfect christian, but that is far from the truth.

Before you were even born God knew you. You are fully known and entirely loved by God in such wonderful glorious ways. God's grace extends beyond our comprehension and what I love about God's love is that we do not have to do anything to make Him love us more or less. Through His precious beloved Son, the Lord Jesus Christ, we are able to receive the love of God within abundance. I am honestly so grateful. How amazing do you feel to know that no matter who you are or what you have done, you are entirely loved by Him. His grace is glowing all over you!

The Flowers Before They Bloom

Whenever you feel unloved or unworthy again, remember this. The source of your identity is not in humans or materialistic things of this world, the source of your precious identity is within the everlasting God. The more you immerse yourself into a deeply intimate relationship with Him, the more you will experience the greatness of His love being showered over your heart. All of a sudden, all the dry places in your life will spring up and be restored.
No longer will you thirst again, no longer will you lack again. For the true lover of your soul is fully in love, interested and invested in you.

I encourage you to fall deeper in love with God and seek His heart like never before. Explore His Word and allow the beauty of truth to penetrate your heart and fill those empty spaces. Be open to the Lord and share with Him all your weaknesses, your wishes, your hopes and desires.

Allow Him to be invited into your life and cultivate a relationship with you as your most treasured, best friend. God is not someone who is afar off, in fact He is very near and close to the brokenhearted.

The Flowers Before They Bloom

He looks after the abandoned, He cherishes and comforts those who are lost and mourning. God is willing and able to take care of you more than you know or could ever understand. Your life and entire destiny is eternally secure in His hands. Never believe the lie nor think you are unworthy to be loved, it is surely far from the truth. Jesus Christ has sacrificed so much for you and is the only person who sees you true worth, beauty and value in its entirety.

The Flowers Before They Bloom

He Will Take Care of You

Beloved Daughter of God,

For many of us, like myself when I first gave my heart to the Lord I found it challenging to truly trust Him with my life and believe that not only is my loving Redeemer, but also my protector and provider. I always grew up in life being told that I will have to take care of myself, and that if I dream for something I will need to work so hard for it because nobody will do it for me. I grew up hearing that nobody will help me, and in this world we go through life alone. So when I cultivated my relationship with God, the more I got to know His heart the more He began to reveal to me that He wishes for me to see Him more as my eternal Heavenly Father who will surely look after me.

There were so many desires in my heart, there still is now. Good desires, visions and dreams of fulfilling the personal calling on my life that God has given to me.

The Flowers Before They Bloom

The desire to get married, the desire to have a successful career, the desire to become confident, healed and whole. I went through life with that narrative in my mind that all this has to be achieved by my own efforts. Then the more I delved deeper into the Word and stronger in my prayer life, I began to understand that the Lord doesn't want us to have the abundant life experience He has called us to have with that ungodly narrative in our minds.

I came to a point where God really had to chasten me and align my mindset to Him and His Word. To truly become as a child again who depends on her Father for everything. Some of you may have been disappointed by your parents during your childhood years, but God, your perfect Father is unlike us as humans. He will never fail you, you are His beloved. His love and grace for you exceeds beyond comprehension. Your mind will not be able to even understand the greatness and weight of how much the Lord is in adoration of you. God is love in itself and He cannot disappoint or lie as you place your trust in Him.

The Flowers Before They Bloom

I believe God wants you to let go of your worries and cares about the things you are desiring for or concerned about. He has everyday of your life already taken care of in His precious hands. All you need to do is be still and know that He is God. He is able to mend and heal every broken place within you, and pour out blessings of the good and pleasant things you've been desiring for. God does want to bless you. That He may be glorified and magnified greatly in your life.

I came to realise that it's truly not the best idea to expect all the good things in my life to come from me. I would become too heavily dependant on myself and would depend on God for nothing. I believe God doesn't want that. He is called Jehovah Jireh for a reason, He is a provider. He is truly able to provide us all that we need and more. Exceedingly and abundantly more than we could as for or imagine. He has a beautiful, generous heart and as you lean in your trust into Him, greater things will spring forth into your life. In Hebrews it says that without placing your faith in God it's impossible to please Him.

The Flowers Before They Bloom

We cannot go through life having faith in our own strength, magnificent miracles and wonders take place as we finally make the choice to let go of our baggages of cares and lay them at His feet for Him to take care of.

Your wonderful provider, your healer and deliverer. There is nothing He cannot do for you. All things work together for the good of those that love the Lord. Whatever it is that you need, He will supply!

You Are Forgiven

Sweet Daughter of God,

Everyone has a past. Everybody. And not everyone's past is pleasant, there are others like myself who have a dark, ugly past that you feel ashamed and guilty to even think about. The enemy loves to make us look backward and think we are unworthy to have a relationship with God. But that's the beauty of God's grace. It doesn't matter what we have done, if we repent genuinely and sincerely with our hearts and believe in the Lord Jesus Christ then we are indeed forgiven.

He cleanses us of our sins with His incorruptible precious blood, He washes us with His Word and nurtures our hearts with His unfailing love.

What's even more beautiful is that He cultivates us to grow to become a better, fruitful person that is blossoming in spirit and in our character to become more like Him.

The Flowers Before They Bloom

So truly, it doesn't matter where you start, what matters is what's in front of you. Christ extends His wings over you gracefully in adoration of you. Because you are precious to God. So precious that He came on this earth to redeem you!! Yes He looked at every bit of your sin and all your mistakes but that did not stop Him from coming to save you.

Nothing will ever separate you from the love of God in Christ Jesus. There is no height, nor depth, nor powers or principalities, neither life nor death that can be able to separate you from His glorious love. Nothing. That also includes your past.

I want to encourage you to immerse yourself in His Word, in prayer in the fullness of His presence. Feel His love for you that is so deep. None can compare to that love. God in His grace doesn't focus on the person who you were, He looks at what He can do in you for you to flourish in your faith in Him and grow to become healed in your heart and whole in your spirit.

The Flowers Before They Bloom

Never look back, look upwards and onwards onto the Lord. Mediate on His Word daily, take up the whole armour of God that you are able to stand against the lies of the enemy. Reach for the sword of the Spirit, which is the Word of God and speak forth the truth of His Word. You have the wonderful victory in Christ Jesus. You are fearfully and wonderfully made. You are more than a conquerer in the Lord and He is holding you close, embracing you in His love throughout every moment of your life.

You are forgiven. There is so much beautiful and glorious things ahead in your life, prosperous plans that God has ordained for you to give you a blossoming future and a hope. He has destined you for great and mighty things. Keep on going, never be discouraged because the Lord is with you always.

He Will Never Leave or Forsake You

Dear Beautiful Daughter of God,

I'm sure many of us have experienced some form of abandonment or disappointment. The experience of having someone close in your life but they left, which resulted in your heart being torn into pieces. I know that aching feeling. The Lord knows that feeling. But His strength is dwelling so potently within you because in courage and resilience, you still stand today. Alive and breathing, God has so many lovely plans and a wonderful purpose for you here. He's not finished with you yet, as you pursue His glorious heart and immerse yourself in precious time with Him, He will draw even closer to you and provide you with the healing, love and affection that you need.

The Lord wants you to get back up on your feet again, with great confidence and security in His love. He knows you may have had some setbacks, disappointments and moments where you have been rejected.

The Flowers Before They Bloom

However there is nothing that you are going through that God is unable to restore. He will restore all you that you lost and every tear that you have shed in the late hours of the night, He has surely seen. He will turn those tears of sorrow into tears of joy. He will replace that feeling of heaviness you've been experiencing for a garment of praise. May your mourning be turned into dancing. For the Lord has His hand on you, firmly upon you in His grace He will not give up on you.

You may have gone through windy storms throughout the seasons of your life, but I encourage you that God has been your anchor and strength. He will continue to support you and keep you stable, secure and taken care of underneath His glorious shadow. Even though others have forsaken you, the Lord has taken you in.

And I know it may get lonely sometimes where it feels as though there's nobody around you, but please remember that even though you cannot see, God is right there next to you holding your hand lovingly in His.

The Flowers Before They Bloom

You are His precious one, too lovely and valuable to be let go. You are cherished and adored, worth much more than rubies or the riches of this world. You have so much value to God and He has promised you that He will never leave.

This is a beautiful time to seek His heart if you haven't already. And if you have, pursue His heart deeper than you ever have before. Be hungry for His Word and thirsty for His presence and you will be filled. Whenever you are feeling down, it's the best thing you can do. Run into the presence of your Father, God Almighty. He will fill your heart with overwhelming joy and your mouth with praise.

You Are Progressing Beautifully

Beautiful Daughter of God,

There is a deceptive narrative that people still have which is that your background determines how fruitful you will be in life. Some people tend to think that because they had a difficult upbringing they will be broken and unsuccessful, or if you've had a series of toxic relationships then there's no hope in expecting to have a wonderful, pleasant marriage someday. Some people believe that our past dictates our future. And who we are will determine where we will go in life. But I believe that's far from the truth.

God has transformed and blossomed the lives of so many people, His glory is seen mightily over the lives of multitudes of people. I will use Queen Esther again as an example. She was a young Jewish, orphan with a heartbreaking past, but the Lord positioned her into royalty and He got the glory from her life.

The Flowers Before They Bloom

There is also Joseph, someone who had a dream but went through pits and prisons to then finally be promoted to become one of the most powerful men in influence within Egypt.
And finally of course, I could never forget someone like King David. The man who came from such humble beginnings, who was a shepherd boy throughout the younger years of his life and being so skilled and gifted with musical instruments. He was then called into the King's presence and eventually was promoted to become the King of Israel himself.
This is so powerful. For it shows that God can flourish a life of excellence and overflow of fruitfulness in the lives of those who didn't even expect it.
As I mentioned earlier before, your past doesn't determine your future. God determines your future. So whatever you are going through now, I encourage you that the Lord can transform your life beautifully within a moment!

However something I realised is that there is usually a process of cultivating our character that has to be done first.

The Flowers Before They Bloom

For every great blessing there has to be a process. Beautiful things don't come out of nowhere. I find that many of us love to try and hide away from the journey and want to just get to the destination.
However life itself is a journey, we must learn to embrace every single moment of it. Like a blossoming flower, or a beautiful butterfly, these lovely things did not turn up this way overnight. There was a process that had to take place. And that's probably what God is doing with you right now.

You may be wondering why certain things haven't happened yet, or you're probably being quite hard on yourself concerning certain things that you're working towards. Whether its trying to be a better person, having a successful career or business, getting into a relationship.. it could be absolutely anything. Preparation and process is necessary for things to go forward. For if you have not been prepared for the blessing how would you be able to handle it?

The Flowers Before They Bloom

I was reminded by someone once that sometimes when we ask the Lord for a blessing that we are not ready for it's similar to a young child asking their father for something like a real car. They are unable to receive such a blessing because they have not been prepared for it. I know you may think you are prepared for certain things, but God knows best. He knows us better than we know ourselves and that's something I truly had to come to reality with.

I used to want everything to go my way and I truly wouldn't understand why God hasn't blessed me with certain things I've been praying for years for! But there is beauty in the process.

God is a God of love and good blessings, but He also loves the process in seeing you bloom in character, maturity and strength to become the person He has called you to be!
I encourage you to do not despise what you're currently experiencing, it's all part of the wonderful process and journey that God is taking you on. You are loved and you are blessed. May you rise in strength and flourish in your faith like never before.

Letter of Love and Encouragement

Throughout your journey with God on healing and transformation, I hope The Flowers Before They Bloom was a blessing to you.

I hope it encouraged you as you felt the warmth and love of the Lord filling and overflowing from within your heart.

My desire is for you to be uplifted with a stirring in your heart to pursue the God's heart more. Thank you for reading, may you be blessed always.

Lots of love,

Devona Fayana

Acknowledgements

To the Lord for never giving up on me and always being faithful and true. You are my heart's anchor and you always keep me safe and sound in your steadfast love. Thank you for sharing your wisdom with me and blossoming me to grow in every area of my life.

To my Mom, for being an amazing mother and always encouraging me in the Lord, staying close by my side throughout every season.

To my Nan, my beautiful grandmother who is now left the earth to be with the Lord. I will always appreciate her for all that she taught me about God and His love for us as I was growing up.

Thank you all.